Александр Скрябин   Alexander Skryabin
(1872–1915)

ПОЛНОЕ СОБРАНИЕ СОЧИНЕНИЙ

Complete Works · Sämtliche Werke
Œuvres complètes

для фортепиано
for piano · für Klavier · pour piano

VIII

Sonatas (II)

Urtext

Редакция · Edited by · Herausgegeben von · Edité par
Victor Yekimovsky
K 264
Könemann Music Budapest

INDEX

I

APPENDIX

II

Соната №6

Sonata No.6

Op.62.
1911 - 12

6

joyeux, triomphant

joyeux

appel
mystérieux

sombre

appel mystérieux

epanouissement de forces mystérieuses

20

Соната №7   Sonata No.7

Op.64.
1911 - 12

K 264

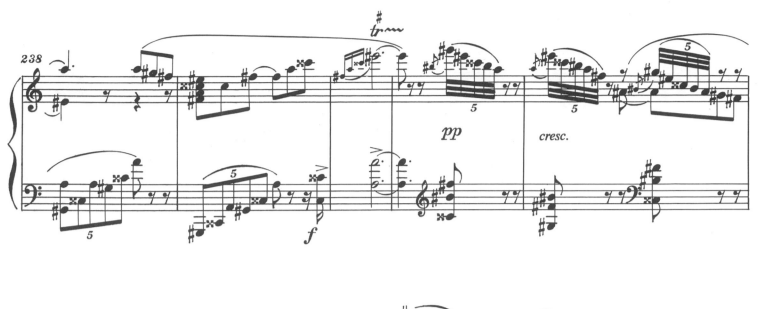

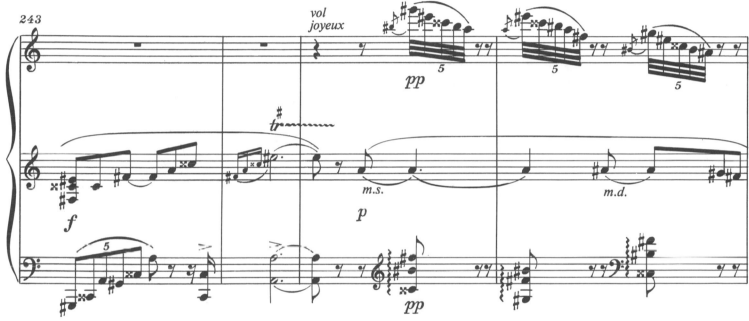

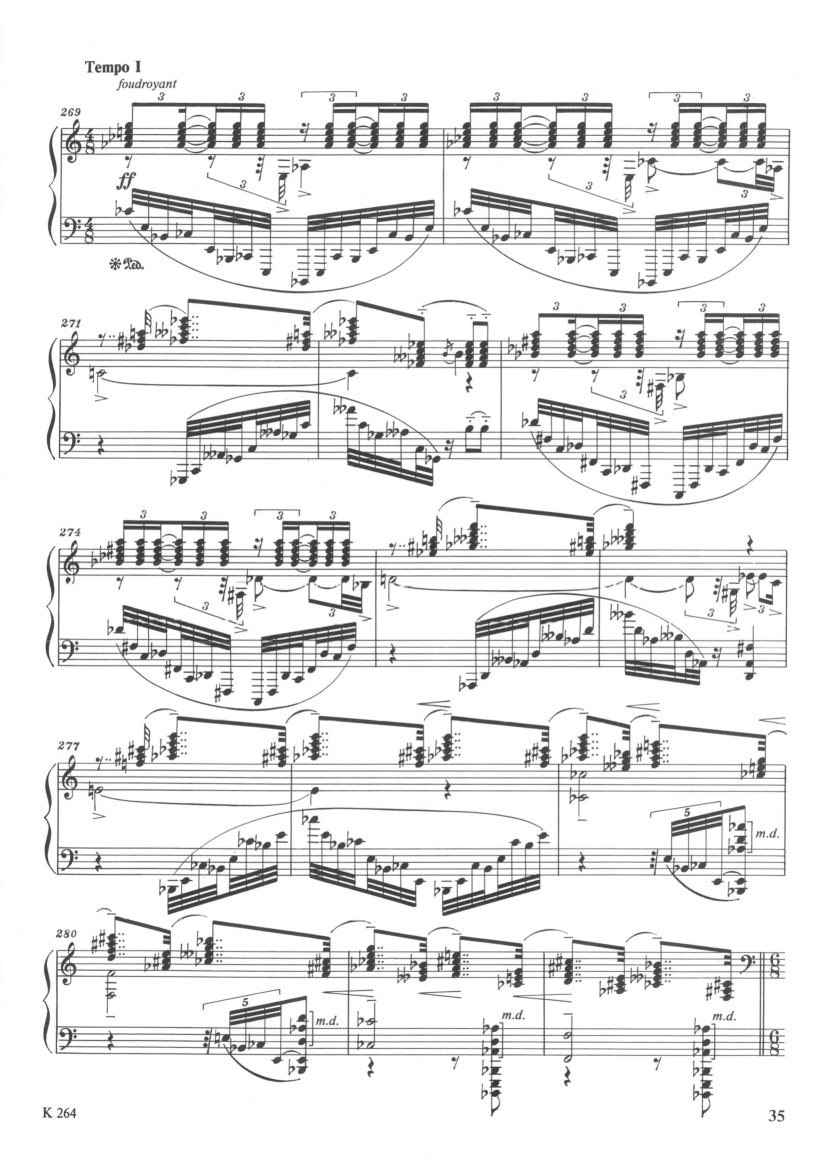

avec une joie débordante

Соната №8   Sonata No.8

Op.66.
1912 - 13

Tragique. Molto più vivo

Соната №9   Sonata No.9

Op.68.
1912 - 13

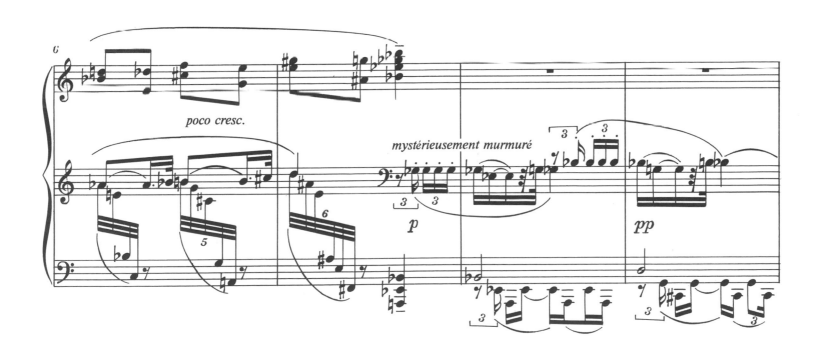

avec une langeur naissante

poco rit.

Molto meno vivo

avec une douceur de plus en plus caressante et empoisonnée

Allegro molto

Соната №10   Sonata No.10

Op.70.
1912 - 13

K 264

Puissant, radieux

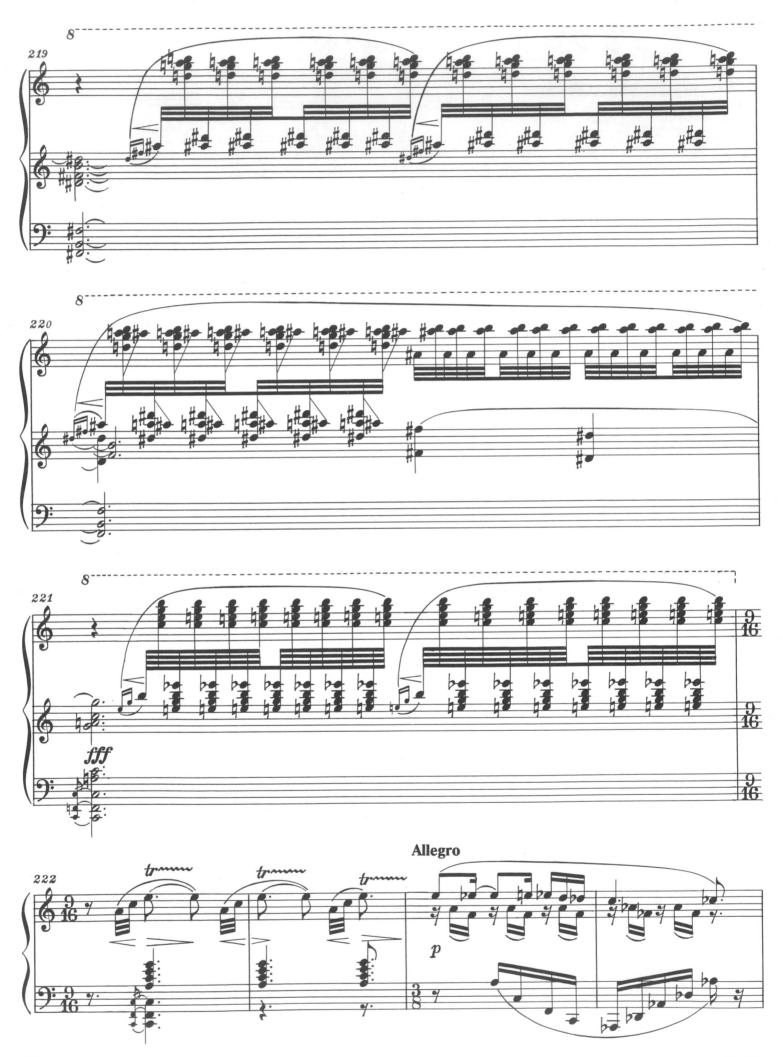

avec élan lumineux vibrant

100

Moderato *avec une douce langueur de plus en plus eteinte*

Notes

The present edition contains the complete works for piano by A. Skryabin in 8 volumes. The eighth volume contains Sonatas Nos. 6–10. The present edition is based on the autograph manuscript and/or first edition(s) of the works. Other editions have also been consulted, whenever justified. Unfortunately the Skryabin archives are not complete; in several cases the autographs have not been found. But all the first editions were proof-read by the composer and all the changes made by the composer in autographs are maintained throughout. Obvious slips of the pen and printing errors have been tacitly corrected. Editorial additions reduced to a minimum appear in square brackets. The composer's peculiarities of notation and original fingering are maintained throughout. All dates are in the Old Style.

Sonata No. 6, op. 62
The autograph is lost. Only a draft survives (SCMMC, estate 31, No. 39).
First edition: Russian Music Publishers (1912).

Page 23, bar 373, upper stave, the note d^5 does not exist on the piano keyboard. Skryabin himself played c^5.

Sonata No. 7, op. 64
The autograph is lost. Only a draft survived (SCMMC, estate 31, No. 44).
First edition: Russian Music Publishers (1912).

Sonata No. 8, op. 66
Autograph: SCMMC, estate 31, No. 55.
First edition: P. Jurgenson (1913).

Page 70, bar 490, upper stave, the autograph and the first edition on the first crotchet of the bar have: ,

which is undoubtely an error. Emended in accordance with the Notes of the edition: A. Skryabin, Sonatas (MUZYKA, 1981).

Sonata No. 9, op. 68
Autograph: SCMMC, estate 31, No. 61.
First edition: Russian Music Publishers (1912).

Sonata No. 10, op.70
Autograph: SCMMC, estate 31, No. 68.
First edition: P. Jurgenson (1913).

Page 93, bar 201, lower stave, the first note in the autograph and the first edition is *G natural*. Emended to *G flat* following the suggestion by Alexander Satz.

ABBREVIATIONS:

1. SCMMC   State Central Museum of Musical Culture (Moscow)
2. CWP   A. Skryabin,Complete works for piano, MUZGIZ,
                vol. I – 1947, vol. II – 1948, vol. III – 1953.

"I would like to have been born as an idea, to fly round whole the world and to fulfil by myself the whole universe. I would like to have been born as a wonderful dream of young life, a motion of sacred inspiration, an impulse of passionate sense". These words were written by Skryabin, a young graduate from the Moscow Conservatory in his album in 1892. Talented pianist and outstanding composer, Skryabin, with his original philosophic ideas, discovered new paths in the development of music.

Alexander Skryabin was born on 25th December 1871 in Old style (6th January 1872 in New style) in Moscow in the house of his grandfather Alexander Skryabin, a retired colonel of the artillery. His father, Nikolai Skryabin, was an expert in Oriental languages and spent most of his life abroad in the diplomatic service. His mother Lyubov Petrovna Skryabina (born Shchetinina) graduated from the St. Petersburg Conservatory in 1866 (class of professor T. Leshetitsky) and was a talented pianist. She gave many recitals in the best halls of St. Petersburg, Moscow and other cities of Russia with great success. She died when Skryabin was still a child and he received his basic musical education mainly from his aunt Lyubov Alexandrovna Skryabina, his father's sister. She later recalled: "Alexander displayed a love for music from when he was in the cradle. At the age of three he could play the piano for long hours although he then played with only one finger. At five he could play with two hands".

In August 1881 he entered the second Moscow Cadet School, afterwards abandoning a military career for music. In 1885 he began to study piano with Nikolai Zverev, who was a famous piano teacher, a pupil of Dubuque. Sergey Rachmaninov, Matvey Presman, Leonid Maximov were his pupils at this period, as well as Skryabin. His fellow pupil, Matvey Presman, later a famous professor of piano, recalled: "Sometimes on Sundays Zverev invited his friends. Skryabin was a frequent visitor to these parties. The first part was a marvellous dinner with imposing food and drink, and the second part was a concert. The performers of the concert were Zverev's pupils, and the audience was the other guests. One of the most honoured members of these parties was P. I. Tchaikovsky".

In 1887 Skryabin entered the Moscow Conservatory, where he studied counterpoint under S. Taneyev and piano under Safonov. He used to play at the students' public concerts with great success. Simultaneously his first piano compositions appeared. In 1892 he graduated from the Moscow Conservatory and was awarded a small gold medal, not large one like Rachmaninov. As a result of conflict with A. Arensky, his professor of composition, Skryabin graduated from the Conservatory only as a pianist, not as a composer.

In summer 1891, before his last year at the conservatory, he began to learn Liszt's transcription of "Don Giovanni" and the oriental fantasy "Islamey" by Balakirev. Not long before these pieces were performed by his fellow student Joseph Levin, and Skryabin decided to reach this level of pianism. His virtuoso capacities were not outstanding and as a result of these studies he damaged his arm. Later Skryabin wrote in his diary: "20 years old: the progressed indisposition of arm ... Providence sends an obstacle to reach the desired aim: splendour, glory ... The first serious failure of life. The first serious meditation: the beginning of analysis. Doubt in impossibility of recovery, but the most gloomy mood. The first serious reflection on a value of life, on religion, on God ...".

In October 1891 Skryabin met at the party a charming girl – Natalya Sekerina. She became his first love. She was about fifteen years old, a beautiful, clever, talented girl.

The beginning of his career after graduating from the conservatory was successful. In 1893 the publishing house of P. Jurgenson published Skryabin's first piano compositions: Valse op. 1, Etude op. 2, Ten mazurkas op. 3, Two nocturnes op 5; they were very popular among amateurs of music. In February 1894 in St. Petersburg, at his recital, Skryabin met for the first time M. P. Belyayev, a very rich timber merchant, a famous amateur of music and patron of the arts. This meeting was very important for Skryabin's career. Belyayev had founded a musical publishing house in Leipzig to popularize new compositions by Russian composers. He offered to pay Skryabin a monthly salary as an advance for his compositions, which he would publish. This was good for the young composer, because he had the opportunity to create. In 1895 Belyayev organized a concert tour to Europe for Skryabin: Germany, Italy, Switzerland. And in the same year Skryabin received a "Becker" grand piano from Belyayev as a present. Belyayev began to publish Skryabin's compositions and payed him very good fees.

At that time he established a close relationship with the St. Petersburg composers Nicolai Rimsky-Korsakov, Anatoly Lyadov and Alexander Glazunov. His music attracted the attention of the famous Russian art critic Vladimir Stasov. Skryabin made a brilliant debut as perfomer of his own works both at home and abroad – in Paris, Belgium, Netherlands and Germany. From 1898 until 1903 he taught piano at the Moscow

Conservatory and reared a number of talented pianists. In those years he became aware of his outstanding gifts and of the high responsibility of his mission as an artist.

The early 1900s were marked by Skryabin's profound interest in philosophy. He made a careful study of works by Spengler, Nietzsche and Fisher. His philosophical views were to a large degree shaped under the influence of the Rector of Moscow University, Sergei Trubetscoy, a prominent philosopher and journalist. The idea of extending the philosophical programme of his music became predominant in Skryabin's mind. The years from 1904 until 1910 were characterized by his tremendous artistic insights and discoveries. During that period Skryabin developed an innovatory idiom, particularly in the field of harmony. He dispensed with the traditional major-minor system and evolved a harmonic style marked by tremendous complexity. This is exemplified in such masterpieces as Symphony No. 3, op. 43, in which he demonstrated his consummate mastery as a symphonist and orchestrator by employing a tremendous orchestra with quadruple woodwind, thus achieving effective tone colours; "The Poem of Extasy", op. 54, based on a programme in verse in which Skryabin proclaimed the triumph of the human will; and the monumental symphonic composition "Prometheus" or The Poem of Fire, scored for very large orchestra, with an important piano part, large mixed wordless chorus, and colour-organ. As Skryabin advanced along the road of musical innovation, his artistic universe became more clearly outlined and his interest in music, past and present, grew more specific. He was no longer infatuated by Chopin. Liszt's music attracted him by its lofty aesthetic and philosophical ideas, and Wagner's works bore resemblance to his own experiments in combining the arts of music, poetry and drama. Skryabin had a critical attitude to contemporary Western trends in music, such as Impressionism and Expressionism, and their representatives Debussy, Schoenberg and R. Strauss.

Skryabin's music gained wide recognition in the first decade of the 20th century. His works were performed by the most celebrated conductors and pianists of his time, among them, Sergey Koussevitzky, Alexander Siloti, Emil Cooper, Willem Mengelberg, Arthur Nikitsch, Sir Henry Wood, Felix Blumenfeld, Josef Levin. He made new acquainances in the musical community. The area of his concert tours considerably expanded. In the season of 1906 – 1907 Skryabin appeared in the USA, where he played his own piano works, while his symphonic compositions were performed under Modest Altschuler with whom Skryabin had studied at the Moscow conservatory, and who had founded the Russian Symphony Orchestra in the USA.

During the last Moscow period of his life (1910 – 1915) Skryabin mixed mainly with a small circle of his close friends, although a large number of visitors, not only musicians, came to see him in his house. In those years Skryabin appeared widely throughout Russia. In the spring of 1910 he went on a tour down the Volga river. He also went on tours abroad, for instance to England in 1914. He developed an engrossing interest in Indian philosophy and had plans to visit India.

His sudden death from blood poisoning occurred on 14th April, 1915. He was buried in Novodevichye cemetery in Moscow. The Russian musical community was deeply affected by his premature death. Concerts in his memory were held in all the large Russian cities.

Skryabin devoted his efforts exclusively to writing instrumental music, for piano or for orchestra. His works include preludes, etudes, impromptu, poems, mazurkas, waltzes, three symphonies, a piano concerto, "The Poem of Extasy", and "Prometheus". Most of his works are based on a programme the aim of which, according to Skryabin, was to create, by means of music, the world filled with sun, a realm of joy, spiritual freedom and extasy: lucid and fragile lyrical images, the embodiment of the ideal, acquired vigour and daring through an extensive development of winged themes and the vehement reiteration of a heroic message. In the last years of his life Skryabin endeavoured to expand the range of music further by harmoniously combining music, words, movement, colour and light, to produce a universal work of art which would have a much stronger impact then a purely musical composition. Similarly other contemporary artists were striving to innovate poetry, theatre and painting. Mention should be made here of the "musical" poetry of the symbolists, of Mikalojus Ciurlions' "musical" paintings, and of the fusion of music, movement and design in Vsevolod Meyerhold's and Alexander Tairov's theatrical experiments. Skryabin's idea of the synthesis of the arts can be discerned in his last grandiose work, "L'acte préalable", which he did not live to complete.

© 1999 for this edition by Könemann Music Budapest Kft.
H-1093 Budapest, Közraktár utca 10.

K 264

Distributed worldwide by
Könemann Verlagsgesellschaft mbH, Bonner Str. 126.
D-50968 Köln

Responsible co-editor: Vladimir Ryabov
Production: Detlev Schaper
Cover design: Peter Feierabend
Technical editor: Dezső Varga

Engraved in Russia

Printed by Kossuth Printing House Co., Budapest
Printed in Hungary

ISBN 963 9059 74 9

KÖNEMANN MUSIC BUDAPEST
April 1999

PÄDAGOGISCHE AUSGABEN
für Klavier
PEDAGOGICAL EDITIONS
for piano

PIANO STEP BY STEP

Alte Tänze – *Early Dances*
Beethoven: 47 Piano Pieces
Einführung in das polyphone Spiel –
Introduction to Polyphonic Playing
Erste Konzertstücke I–II–III–IV
First Concert Pieces I–II–III–IV
Etüden
Haydn: 23 Piano Pieces
Mozart: 44 Piano Pieces
Sonatinen I–II–III
Vierhändige Klaviermusik – *Works for
Piano Duet I–II–III*

IN VORBEREITUNG – *IN PREPARATION*
Grieg: 37 Piano Pieces

FAVOURITE PIANO STUDIES

Carl Czerny:

100 Übungsstücke – *100 Exercises,*
Op. 139
Die Schule der Geläufigkeit – *The
School of Velocity,* Op. 299

Kunst der Fingerfertigkeit – *The Art of
Finger Dexterity* I–II, Op. 740

IN VORBEREITUNG – *IN PREPARATION*
160 Übungsstücke – *160 Exercises*

Pekka Vapaavuori–Hannele Hynninen:

Der Barockpianist – *The Baroque Pianist*

FAVOURITES for piano

Amazing Grace & Other
  Popular American Songs
American Classical Songs I–II
Favourite Piano Classics I–IV
Favourite Opera Classics I–II (Mozart)
Favourite Opera Classics III–IV (Verdi)
Favourite Opera Classics V–VI (Italian
  Composers)
Scott Joplin: Ragtimes
Spirituals
Johann Strauss: Walzer
When the Saints Go Marchin' in...
  and other Popular American Songs
IN VORBEREITUNG – *IN PREPARATION*
Favourite Ballet Classics I–II
  (Tchaikovsky: Schwanensee,
  Dornröschen, Nußknacker)

KLAVIERAUSZÜGE
VOCAL SCORES

Johann Sebastian Bach:
Johannes-Passion
Matthäus-Passion
Weihnachts-Oratorium
Magnificat

Georg Friedrich Händel:
Der Messias

Wolfgang Amadeus Mozart:
Requiem

IN VORBEREITUNG – *IN PREPARATION*
Giovanni Pergolesi:
Stabat Mater

Joseph Haydn:
Nelson Messe

KAMMERMUSIK
CHAMBER MUSIC

Cello Meets Piano I–II
Flute Meets Piano I–II
Violin Meets Piano I–II

GITARRE – *GUITAR*

Fernando Sor – Matteo Carcassi
Klassische Etüden – *Classical Studies*

Francisco Tárrega
Originalkompositionen – *Original
Compositions*

IN VORBEREITUNG – *IN PREPARATION*
Mauro Giuliani: Variationen
Luis Milán: Fantasien